"Buy this book, apply these secrets, and your prosperity will be assured."

-- Dan McComas, President, Dan McComas Associates, Marketing & Management Consultants.

"This breakthrough book, based on the ideas of a forgotten genius, will help smart marketers increase their effectiveness a minimum of fivefold."

-- Bruce David, publisher of "Starting Smart."

"The principles are sound and sensible, and guaranteed to help any business person make more money. Since 99.9% of businesses don't use them, anyone putting the seven lost secrets to work will gain an unbelievable edge over the competition."

-- Bob Bly, author of 18 business books, including *Selling Your Services.*

"One of the most revealing works ever! I literally couldn't put it down. There are 'life and business' success lessons in each chapter."

-- Jim Chandler, President, VistaTron.

The Seven Lost Secrets of Success

by Joe Vitale

ISBN 1-881760-00-6

Published by VistaTron, 222 Ohio Street, Ashland, OH 44805-0321. Discounts for bulk orders are available. Call (419) 281-3927.

For more information about the marketing, speaking and writing services of Joe Vitale, please write or call: Joe Vitale, PO Box 300792, Houston, TX 77230-0792. Phone: (281) 999-1110. Fax: (281)999-1313.

First Edition: August 14, 1992

Library of Congress Catalog Card Number: 92-90948

Printed in the U.S.A.

Printed On Recycled Paper

"One never knows, when he enters an elevator or tears open an envelope or picks up the telephone, what new trick of fortune may be about to be played. Every day is a new series of adventures; around the next corner may lie the event that will change a whole career."

-- Bruce Barton, 1928

Other Works By Joe Vitale

Turbocharge Your Writing

Zen And The Art Of Writing

Hypnotic Writing Skills

The Joy Of Service (with Ron McCann)

About Bruce Barton

"The man has genius."
          -- *New York Herald Tribune*, 1927

"The Prophet of Advertising."
          -- *Advertising Digest*, 1949

"Million Dollar Ad Man."
          -- *Chicago Daily News*, 1944

"The modern philosopher for millions."
          -- *Tribune Newshawks*, 1945

"He should be advertising's Man Of The Century."
          - *Printers' Ink*, 1961

"Bruce Barton breathed inspiration..."
          -- *The Advertising News*, 1924

CONTENTS

Dedication

For **Marian**...

the loving sunshine who has

supported me every step of the way,

no matter what the project,

or the outcome of it.

Acknowledgments

Several people helped me create this book.

Thanks to Mrs. Caples, wife of the late copywriting king John Caples, for sharing a moment by phone that made my eyes well up in tears. She knew Bruce Barton through her husband's work and gave me a couple of excellent leads for background material. I will not forget talking to her.

Thanks to Greg Manning, Jim King, and Scott Hammaker, three rare friends. Their encouragement and stimulating ideas have always managed to somehow keep my projects alive and me moving forward.

Thanks to Dan Starr for his initial research and Bruce Barton bibliography.

Thanks to the Houston Public Library for answering my questions and hunting down copies of old books through their miraculous interlibrary loan system.

Thanks to Colleen of Colleen's Books, for her amazing ability to locate out-of-print books on a wide variety of topics. She's been a reliable resource for nearly 20 years.

Thanks to Harold Miller and Christine Schelshorn, of The State Historical Society of Wisconsin, for their aid in locating specific Bruce Barton materials.

Thanks to John B. Wingate of the International Center For The Disabled for granting permission for me to use excerpts from Bruce Barton's writings in this book.

Several people read earlier versions of this book, or just encouraged me to keep writing, and gave helpful feedback or advice: Murray Raphel, Herschell Gordon Lewis, Debbie Zimmerman, Jerry Twentier, Tina Nokes, Stuart Nokes, Claudette Manning, Carol Marashi, Bob Bly, Dan McComas, Milton Ward, Douglas Norment, Judith Barton Dennis, Cliff Leonard, Mark Weisser, Jim Chandler, Martin Parris, Tillie Wier, Lyle Steele, Marquita Anderson, and Deborah Healon all deserve a round of applause.

Jean at the River Oaks Book Store helped me brainstorm a worthy title for the book.

And thanks, of course, for Dottie Walters' friendship, support, ideas, and for her touching foreword.

This book has obviously been a team effort.

Joe Vitale
Houston
1992

"In every human being, whether emperor or cowboy, prince or pauper, philosopher or slave, there is a mysterious *something* which he neither understands nor controls. It may lie dormant for so long as to be almost forgotten; it may be so repressed that the man supposes it is dead. But one night he is alone in the desert under the starry sky; one day he stands with bowed head and damp eyes beside an open grave; or there comes an hour when he clings with desperate instinct to the wet rail of a storm-tossed boat, and suddenly out of the forgotten depths of his being this mysterious *something* leaps forth. It over-reaches habit; it pushes aside reason, and with a voice that will not be denied it cries out its questionings and its prayer."

-- Bruce Barton, *What Can A Man Believe?*, 1927

FOREWORD

by Dottie Walters

(Dottie is the author of several books, including *Speak & Grow Rich!* and *Never Underestimate The Selling Power Of A Woman.* She is also President of Walters International Speakers Bureau, and Chairman of the Board for the American Association of Professional Consultants.)

What a wonderful book! I am delighted that my friend Joe Vitale has written about a great man who profoundly influenced my life. When I met Bruce Barton, I needed his help badly. I had begun my small advertising business on foot, pushing my two babies before me on a rickety baby stroller with pillows tied on with rope.

There were few sidewalks in the chicken ranching community of Baldwin Park. When the stroller wheel kept coming off, I hit it back on with the heel of my shoe, then picked up the cardboard I had stuffed inside to cover the holes, shook it out and stuck it back in. My husband needed my help. I was determined that we would not lose our home in the recession.

14

During high school my English teacher had pulled me out of regular English and insisted I take journalism. How I loved it. I worked after school and on weekends in the bakery of a midnight market. After I scrubbed the floors and washed the cases, I wrote articles and poems for "The Moor," our high school newspaper. So, when we needed money so badly, I thought of the newspaper.

There were certainly no jobs in that recession period. I persuaded The Baldwin Park Bulletin to sell me advertising space at half price. Then I called on the merchants and sold them the space at full price, adding my copy to their products as a shoppers column I called "Window Wishing." The difference was my profit.

"I write from the customers viewpoint" I told them enthusiastically. But I had no college. I felt so unprepared in that man's world. But I did have one wonderful thing to help me with my fledging business: The Baldwin Park Library. Every evening I would run over and pick up books on advertising, business and sales.

It was there I met Bruce Barton. I read all his books, and read them again. I heard his voice in my mind. Uplifting, teaching, showing me how.

Then one day the Publisher of The Baldwin Park Bulletin handed me a notice from the Advertising Association. There was to be a meeting in San Francisco. Bruce Barton would be the speaker!

It took a lot of thinking and planning to put the money together and to arrange for baby sitters in order to go. But I made it. I stuffed apples and a package of crackers in my briefcase because I did not have money for meals. I didn't stay overnight. I just came to hear Mr. Barton.

He had white hair, a slight build, and told stories that enchanted the audience. He said he based his advertising business on two things:

First was a Bible verse: **"Agree with your adversary early."** He explained that the customer relaxes when you see their side of the situation. That when you really understand what your customer wants, then it is so easy to show them that your product or service is just what they need to get it. **"Your job is to be the buyer's assistant,"** Mr. Barton said.

Second he asked the audience if we remembered the 3rd verse of "Mary Has A Little Lamb." Everyone knew the first verse, a few the 2nd, but no one could say the 3rd. He recited it as the second great principle of his advertising business:

> **"Why does the lamb love Mary so?"**
> **The eager children cry**
> **"Because Mary loves the lamb, you**
> **know,"**
> **The teacher did reply."**

I remember that I jumped as he hit the lectern with a loud bang as he said that 3rd line. Then he said, **"It is about time we quit trying to shear these sheep - and start loving them a little bit!"**

I saw immediately that Mr. Barton meant that we must see things from our customers' eyes. To care for their interests, to help them. Because of his teaching, I built my small advertising business into all of Southern California, hired and trained 285 employees who sold over 4,000 continuous contract advertising accounts. We had four offices. My customers brought me other customers. Mr. Barton's principles were the foundation of my business then, and they still are.

But on that day in San Francisco when I was so young, uneducated and yearning for knowledge and help for my tiny start-up business, I waited until his speech was over. It took a long time for everyone to shake his hand, and finally leave. Then I walked up to Mr. Barton thinking "How can I tell him that he is my teacher?"

I only had a moment with him. I reached out my hand to him. He took it in both of his. I looked into his kind eyes and said, "I am the one who HEARD you."

Bruce Barton replied, **"You are the one I came for."**

Bruce Barton at 74 (1960?)
(Photo Courtesy AP/World Wide Photos)

"In 1833 a clerk in the patent office at Washington handed in his resignation.

"There was no more need for a job like his (he wrote). Every possible invention had been conceived and patented: there was nothing left to invent.

"In 1833---and nothing left to invent! Before the railroads had spanned the continent! Before electricity lighted our streets and moved our cars! Before the telephone, or the wireless, or the steamshovel, or the dynamo! At the very threshold of the greatest period of mechanical advance that the world has ever known, this young man threw up his hands...

"...the world, with all its times of trouble, still moves ahead. No man can play a big part in the world who does not believe in the future of the world..."

-- Bruce Barton, *It's A Good Old World*, 1920

HOW I DISCOVERED THE LOST SECRETS

"There is no substitute for love."
-- Bruce Barton, 1953

The Ultimate Guru

Business is a great teacher.

It makes you take risks, go for your dreams, face fears, handle your emotions, deal with difficult people, and learn balance. You don't have to do any weird workshops or sign up for any therapy sessions. Go into business and you'll be enrolled in the greatest seminar of all time. And it happens every day, every where, to every one. You can't avoid it.

Though I've done self-help retreats, practiced meditation, walked on fire, and hunted for my inner self, nothing ever compares to the day by day challenges of being in business. It's the ultimate guru. It shows you your fears and challenges you to go past them. It shows you your dreams and challenges you to attain them.

Not too many people talk about business in this way. I thought I was alone in my belief that business could challenge us to be our best, and for a long time I kept silent. But then, while researching advertising methods from the 1920's through 1940's, I found a kindrid spirit from an earlier time...

The Messiah of Business

Bruce Barton lived from 1886 to 1967---from after the Civil War right up to the Vietnam War. Though Barton had a ringside seat for most of our century's greatest events, few remember him today. He has somehow fallen through the cracks of history.

When I tried to learn more about Barton, I hit road-blocks. Few remembered him. His own advertising firm kept quiet when I asked for information. I couldn't find his relatives, anyone who knew him, or anyone who wanted to tell me anything about him. I began to suspect a cover-up of some sort. For a man who ate with Presidents, made history, and led our country on a quest for prosperity, it seemed odd that he was now forgotten.

I decided to do some investigating.

I couldn't believe what I found.

The Man Everyone Knows

Bruce Barton was so famous that in 1938 an envious fellow wrote, "Almost every day there is a story about a man named Barton. Barton says, Barton suggests, Barton shakes hands, Barton laughs, Barton sneezes. It's Barton, Barton, Barton everywhere."

As an author Barton penned many books, including a novel, several volumes of inspiring essays, and the 1925 best-seller *The Man Nobody Knows*. It was this book that made Barton's name a household word. In it he declared that Jesus was the founder of modern business.

The book set an entire nation on a path of service. When Bobbs-Merrill published the book in 1925, they felt it might sell 500 to 1,000 copies. To everyone's surprise (including the author's), the book shot to fourth place on the best seller list in 1925 and was in first place by 1926. It's still in print today.

Written by a minister's son who was also a prominent businessman, *The Man Nobody Knows* made Barton, at least in the roaring twenties, "the man everybody knew."

Barton had contact with every President and every Republican presidential candidate of the mid-twentieth century. He was an enemy of Franklin D. Roosevelt (and FDR openly said so). Barton was also one of the first men in American history to use the media to promote a presidential candidate (Coolidge). At one point Barton, a congressman in the 1930's, was named as a potential presidential candidate.

The Second B In BBDO

As a businessman Barton helped develop the advertising profession. He is the second "B" in BBDO (the famous Batten, Barton, Durstine and Osborn agency). Though Barton was more interested in being a journalist, and only wanted to work in advertising part-time, he helped make BBDO the largest ad agency in the world in the 1940's. Barton created some of the greatest ads in American history, including several to end war (they were never used).

Because of his fame as a writer and businessman, Barton also knew pioneering business leaders, including Andrew Carnegie and Henry Ford. He was the first to help these giants use advertising to promote their goods.

And as a philanthropist Barton used his skills to help many well-known organizations, from the American Heart Association and the United Negro College Fund to the Salvation Army (he coined their slogan "A man is down, but he's never out").

Barton's views, revealed in his books, articles and

speeches, shaped our culture. He was a visionary who predicted television before it was invented. He was a revolutionary who supported Jews and Blacks and Women. He was an optimist who believed in prosperity during the Depression. He was a national leader who helped middle class America adjust to a more modern era. He was the original motivational speaker who created inspirational talks that are still often referred to even today.

Due to World Wars, the Great Depression, and personal tragedies, Barton's popularity weakened. Today few recall him or his startling message.

Business Can Save The World

Barton believed business would save the world. He was a deeply religious man who characterized himself as a Quaker spiritually. But he never felt that heaven would "come all at once." Barton believed that business would help create a heaven on earth.

In 1924 he said, **"...the millennium, if it is ever coming, is coming through the larger increase and service of business."**

At a visit to the White House Barton told President Calvin Coolidge, **"Business is the hope of the world. Give it a free hand under proper supervision and it will bring in the millennium."**

Despite his colorful life, there has never been a biography of Barton (except for a few unpublished dissertations) or a study of his ground-breaking ideas.
Until now.

Secrets To Success Revealed

I believe, like Barton, that responsible actions in business can help us create a life where everyone has a chance for peace, happiness, growth, and prosperity.

This book won't examine Barton's life. Instead, my focus is on Barton's success strategies and on how you can use them today. My belief is that Barton's success at promotion and marketing---his success in *all* areas of life--- was due to these timeless strategies.

Though Barton himself never put his secrets into book form---and though his eyes would probably pop open in surprise while reading this book---I'll stand by what I write. I've studied Barton's life, letters, writings, and ads. I've discovered a set of seven secrets which I feel Barton used, consciously or not, to create his most successful campaigns.

Though one or two of the "lost secrets" are similar to practices used today, you can quickly see that Barton went straight to the heart with his strategies. Barton went for a more global impact.

He didn't write an ad to sell a product; he wrote literary vignettes packed with emotion that reveal

25

how a business transforms life as we know it.

More than that, Barton's ideas provide a fresh and lively approach to promotion, publicity and prosperity; one that goes far beyond any existing methods.

The Seven Lost Secrets Of Success explains and illustrates each of Barton's secrets. It also includes questions and guidelines so you can use the seven strategies to promote yourself or your own business and attain lasting success and prosperity.

Lost 65 Years?

Were Barton's secrets really "lost"?

Yes.

Today I went to the library to look up three famous (once famous) people: Bruce Barton, Helen Woodward and Elmer Wheeler. Barton is the subject of this book; Woodward was a pioneer feminist and female copywriter in the 1920's; Wheeler was a nationally known sales trainer and speaker.

Yet I'll bet you never heard of any of them before today. (If it makes you feel better, the library hadn't heard of them either!)

Why not? What happened to these once great people?

Barton was once a household name. Why doesn't anyone remember him?

26

Woodward made headlines for her protests and ad copy (she was the first to advertise Brady's famous Civil War photos). Why don't we know her name today?

Wheeler wrote best selling books and created a movement of people "selling sizzle, not steak." Why is Wheeler forgotten, too?

What happened?

I believe we are so caught up with what's "new" that we forget about what works. History hasn't forgotten Barton, Woodward or Wheeler. *We* have. Our information age is so constipated with new ideas, new facts, new reports, new studies, new books, new *news*, that we can't possibly retain yesterday's news.

That's a costly mistake. When we forget the tried and true methods, we are forced to relearn them through trial and error (usually a lot of the latter).

Barton had some sensational ideas (so did Woodward and Wheeler, but that's another book). Because we let old knowledge get replaced with new information, we've lost some major secrets to success.

That's why the secrets in this book are "lost secrets."

We've let them get buried.

I simply found them while digging around in old books.

They've benefited me.

Now they can benefit you.

27

Results Guaranteed

These lost secrets work. And I can prove it.

I've tested Barton's strategies in my own life. They have given me money, happiness, credibility, a feeling of self worth, and a sense of contributing to all mankind.

I've seen my clients use these secrets (some knowingly, others by luck), and I've seen them prosper. Their stories, as well as my own, will be shared with you as you turn the pages of this book.

Use these secrets and you will create a legendary, electrifying, prosperous and unshakable business---a business that just might help bring in the millennium the "messiah of business" had hoped for several decades ago.

"Many wealthy men have purchased newspapers with the idea of advancing their personal fortunes, or bringing about some political action in which they have a private interest. Such newspapers almost invariably fail...The public has a sixth sense for detecting insincerity; they know instinctively when words ring true."
-- Bruce Barton, *The Man Nobody Knows*, 1925

From a 1924 radio broadcast:

"Those of you who were brought up on the Bible will recall the account of Joseph's very remarkable business career. It tells how he left his country under difficulties and, coming into a strange country, he rose, through his diligence, to become the principal person in the state, second only to the King.

"Now, my friends, the Biblical narrative brings us to that point---the point where Joseph had made a great success and was widely advertised throughout the country---it brings us up to the climax of his career and then it hands us an awful jolt. Without any words of preparation or explanation, it says bluntly:

'And Joseph died, and there arose a new King in Egypt which knew not Joseph.'

"Now that sentence is one of the most staggering lines which has ever been written in a business biography. Here was a man so famous that everybody knew him and presto, a few people die, a few new ones are born, and nobody knows him. The tide of human life has moved on...

29

"Now, my friends, let us apply that story to modern business. An hour ago there were in this country sick, in bed, several thousand old folks. It is perhaps indelicate for me to refer to that fact, but it is a fact....In this single hour which has just passed, those old folks have died, and all the good-will which advertising has built up in their minds has died with them---all the investment made by that past advertising has gone on into another world where the products are not for sale.

"And in this same hour another thing---equally staggering---has happened. There have been born into this country several thousand lusty boys and girls to whom advertised products mean no more than the Einstein theory. They do not know the difference between a Mazda Lamp and a stick of Wrigley's chewing gum. Nobody has ever told them that Ivory Soap floats or that children cry for Castoria...

"The tramp of human feet is ceaseless across the stage of time...For every day and every hour the king---which is the public---dies; and there arises a new king which knows not Joseph."

-- Bruce Barton

WHY YOU MUST ADVERTISE

--- NO MATTER WHAT YOU DO

"You can't advertise today and quit tomorrow. You're not talking to a mass meeting. You're talking to a parade."
-- Bruce Barton, 1930

Just Try Stopping

"You are going to have national advertising whether you want it or not!" declared Bruce Barton.

U.S. Steel had decided to stop their national advertising. Barton went to Pittsburgh to confront the managers. He told them they could cancel their advertising if they wanted but that a different kind of

31

advertising would continue.

"It is the advertising given you by politicians with axes to grind...by newspapers that hope to build circulation by distorting your acts...by all other operators in the field of public opinion, some unfriendly and some merely misinformed."

Then Barton hit them with a thunderbolt.

"Can you afford to take the risk of having all your advertising emanate from sources beyond your control?"

U.S. Steel renewed their advertising campaigns.

Your True King

Your customer is king. (And if you are working for a boss, your boss is your customer.)

But your customers and clients do not know what you can do for them unless you tell them.

But you must also KEEP telling them.

Every day a new set of customers appears. A new generation is born. Children become buying adults. Adults switch jobs, develop new interests and lifestyles, and develop new needs and desires.

If you do not let these people know about you and your services, they will not know to call you. They will go to whoever they have read about, heard about, or seen advertised. These new buyers will be the new king and they will not know of you.

Either advertise and continue to advertise or a new breed of customers will arise who will ignore you for one simple reason: they won't know you exist.

In 1920 Bruce Barton wrote, **"You think that you have told your story to the world, and that therefore your task is done. I tell you that overnight a new world has been born that has never heard your story."**

You can offer the best service....the lowest prices...free incentives for every man, woman, and child that walks through your doors....but if no one knows of you and your business, no one will come.

"Elias Howe invented the sewing machine but he could not get women to buy it," Barton said in a 1934 speech. **"He lived in poverty, and was reduced to the ignominy of attending his wife's funeral in borrowed clothes. A whole generation of women who might have had their work made easier by his invention lived without its service because there was no advertising to tell them about it."**

And consider Mozart. He wrote the world's greatest music, yet died penniless. Those who followed him, who knew how to advertise, grew wealthy by marketing Mozart's works.

You can be the best worker...the smartest in your field...a person who has won awards for your dedication and excellence....but if you don't somehow let people know about your talents, they won't ever call you or ask for your help.

Note this: When the Great Depression of 1929 rocked America, most companies stopped all their advertising. It seemed like a logical move. But many of the companies who continued to advertise are *still around today!*

There's no way around it.

You MUST advertise.

How To Advertise

I get a lot of mail.

It's amazing to see so many people wasting their money on advertising that doesn't work. It makes me gag. The ads, though often creative, don't get results. The flyers all look alike. The sales letters are impotent. Yet people keep dumping their money into this "advertising" and they keep praying for results.

Eventually they go bankrupt and a new advertiser shows up to offer the same product or service in the same limp way. After a while they fold and someone else comes along. And so it goes....Since the process keeps going, few ever stop to ask if the efforts are actually working.

It's time for a change.

This book will help you promote yourself (or your business) in new, surprising and effective ways----ways already tested decades ago by a man who used the methods to promote legendary businessmen, like Henry Ford and Andrew Carnegie, and even U.S. Presidents, like Calvin Coolidge and Dwight Eisenhower.

Now it's your turn.

The following secrets will help you achieve lasting prosperity and success. You'll still have to design ads that get attention and write letters that get results, but you'll have the edge over everyone else.

You'll have the forgotten secrets of an advertising legend---a man who was prosperous and successful in all areas of life---on your side.

"Advertising is the very essence of democracy. An election goes on every minute of the business day across the counters of hundreds of thousands of stores and shops where the customers state their preferences and determine which manufacturer and which product shall be the leader today, and which shall lead tomorrow."

-- Bruce Barton, 1955

"Here is an important distinction that many people overlook:

"God made the world; but He does not make *your* world.

"He provides the raw materials, and out of them every man selects what he wants and builds an individual world for himself.

"The fool looks over the wealth of material provided, and selects a few plates of ham and eggs, a few pairs of trousers, a few dollar bills--and is satisfied.

"The wise man builds his world out of wonderful sunsets, and thrilling experiences, and the song of the stars, and romance and miracles.

"Nothing wonderful ever happens in the life of a fool...an electric light is simply an electric light; a telephone is only a telephone---nothing unusual at all.

"But the wise man never ceases to wonder how a tiny speck of seed, apparently dead and buried, can produce a beautiful yellow flower. He never lifts a telephone receiver or switches on an electric light without a certain feeling of awe."

-- Bruce Barton, *More Power To You*, 1920

SECRET #1:

REVEAL THE BUSINESS NOBODY KNOWS

"In the long run no individual prospers beyond the measure of his faith." -- Bruce Barton, 1921

A Nation Of Steel

Bruce Barton dug deep to find how a business served a global need or contributed to the growth of the country.

When he and Roy Durstine landed the United States Steel Corporation account in 1935, Barton helped whip up an ad that made history. He said Andrew Carnegie **"...came to a land of wooden towns...and left a nation of steel."**

This type of strategy changed the perspective of

37

everyone. People were no longer buying a product called steel; they were supporting a mission to improve the lifestyle of a nation.

How does your business serve life? How do you contribute to the improvement of lives?

You have to look past the obvious. You may be running a hamburger stand. But are you just selling burgers? Aren't you doing something more---maybe keeping people alive and healthy so they can enjoy their lives and be happier?

How You Can Live Forever

I help people write books. But books aren't my only product. I am in the business of giving *immortality.*

Let me explain:

A book is a way for you to live forever. When you write a book, you put yourself in that book. And you also create something that will live beyond you. Just look at the man we are talking about: Bruce Barton. He died in 1967. But his writings have touched me (and now you) from beyond his grave.

Barton used this tactic to help him write his most famous book.

The Man Nobody Knows made Jesus alive for millions of people. Most people thought (and still think) of Jesus as a sad, wimpy type of savior. But

Barton said Jesus was physically strong from being a carpenter, healthy from walking in the open air every day, popular because He was invited to parties and attracted little kids, and a wise leader because He took 12 unknown men (fishermen!) and made them "salesmen" for His organization---a business that has spanned the globe and touched everyone for thousands of years.

Barton wrote in 1920, **"He (Jesus) was at a wedding party...The wine had given out. So He performed His first miracle. Just to save a hostess from embarrassment---and He thought it worth a miracle. Just to save a group of simple folk from having their hour of joy cut short---it was for such a cause, He thought, that His divine power had been intrusted to Him."**

Nobody ever told ME that before! I now see Jesus with new eyes because of Barton's explanation. Barton revealed the man I never knew.

The Advertising Nobody Knows

Barton also used this strategy on his own profession.

When people complained that advertising was misleading or corrupt, Barton responded by "revealing the business nobody knows."

The late John Caples, author and friend of

Barton's, once wrote in his diary:

"...(Barton) took the profession of advertising and told what wonders it is accomplishing in improving living standards---how it is forwarding the progress of the human race---how it is really a noble profession."

Barton himself said, **"If advertising is sometimes long winded, so is the United States Senate. If advertising has flaws, so has marriage."**

Elsewhere Barton said, **"As a profession advertising is young; as a force it is as old as the world. The first words uttered, 'Let there be light,' constitute its character. All nature is vibrant with its impulse."**

What Barton did was "reframe" the way people viewed his profession. And it worked. His agency became one of the largest in the world.

The President Nobody Knows

When Barton was nominated as a candidate for the U.S. Presidency, he wrote an article for *Cosmopolitan* magazine (1932) which "revealed the President nobody knows."

Most of us consider the President's job to be high-risk, high-stress, high-profile; a controversial and demanding position. Not Barton. He said one of his first official acts would be to buy a horse and join two golf clubs. He wrote:

"The President should never be tired or worried. He should be fresh, clear-minded, full of power and decision. Thus, when his two or three big opportunities arise, he will be prepared to speak the word or perform the act that will fire the imagination of the country."

Bruce Barton went on to say that our Presidents have never been very relaxed. Barton revealed a new President---one nobody ever imagine before---a President who was human.

Though Barton was not elected President, his unique campaign strategy made him more real---and more memorable and endearing---to thousands of people who never knew him.

What People Really Want

The way to perform this first strategy is to think of what people really want.

Cosmetic companies don't sell lipstick; they sell romance (and sex). They know women want to love and be loved. Lipstick is a device to attain it. To "reveal the business nobody knows" a cosmetics firm would focus on the romance and sex derived from using their product.

People want:

41

* security   * sex   * power * immortality * wealth

* happiness * safety * health * recognition * love

How do you (or your business) deliver any of those essential needs?

I mentioned a hamburger stand earlier. Instead of focusing on hamburgers, what if the owner started selling "health"? He could bill his business as the first hamburger stand that caters to your health. He could say, "Our burgers will give you energy and vitamins" or something to that effect. He could "reveal the business nobody knows."

Most people sell what they have in front of them. In other words, if you're selling a shirt, you show the shirt. But a way to "reveal the shirt nobody knows" is to show how the shirt satisfies a more deep-seated desire. Maybe the shirt is made of special material that allows your skin to breathe, thereby giving you health. Maybe the shirt is so attractive that it draws members of the opposite sex, thereby giving you romance. You have to look deeper than the obvious.

Take baking soda. Arm & Hammer has us putting their product on our toothbrushes and in our refrigerators. They are clever people. They keep revealing other uses for their baking soda. But Bruce Barton would have gone further and shown how the powder served the world. Had Barton handled the Arm & Hammer baking soda account, we'd be crop-dusting the planet with the stuff to clear the air of pollution.

When Bruce Barton was handed the Steel account, he could have written a relatively good ad that said "Carnegie Steel is the best in the business."

Instead, Barton looked deeper. He wanted to reveal how the steel business served the more basic needs of people. As a result he came up with the now famous ad (listed in the book, *The 100 Greatest Advertisements Of All Time*): Andrew Carnegie "...came to a land of wooden towns...and left a nation of steel."

The War Nobody Knows

Barton hated war.

He lived through our country's worst wars---from both World Wars right up to the Vietnam War. He knew it was a hopeless activity. **"Nobody can win,"** he said.

In 1932 he created a series of advertisements to "reveal the war nobody knows." He wanted to drive home the costs and pains of war. He wanted to awaken people to the tragic reality of war. Barton knew that future wars would involve airplanes, big business, and even chemicals. And he wanted to stop it by advertising "this HELL!" One of his ads read:

SO THE LUSITANIA WENT DOWN

Well, what of it?

"What of it?" you cry. "The whole world was shocked. For days the newspapers talked of nothing else."

Well, but what of it? After all, it was a little thing.

How many Lusitanias would have to go down to carry all the dead and missing soldiers and the dead civilians of the great World War?

One Lusitania a day.

For a year.

For ten years.

For 25 years.

For 50 years.

One Lusitania a day for 70 years, or one a week, beginning nearly a century before the discovery of America by Columbus and continuing to the present hour.

That is the number of Lusitanias that would be required to carry the dead. The dead of all nations who died in the war.

****

That ad and four others were used as illustrations in Barton's 1932 article (*before* World War II) in *American* magazine. But the ads never ran. And the country's failure to listen to Bruce Barton's plea to "reveal the war nobody knows" allowed further horrors of history to occur.

The Gasoline Nobody Knows

At a 1925 talk to the American Petroleum Institute, Barton told his audience they weren't selling gasoline at all.

"My friends it is the juice of the fountain of eternal youth that you are selling. It is health. It is comfort. It is success. And you have sold it as a bad smelling liquid at so many cents a gallon. You have never lifted it out of the category of a hated expense."

Barton explained his shocking position with a story about Jacob, who's poor immigrant parents had no gas and had to live in a dingy neighborhood under the shadow of ugly smoke (coal) stacks.

"Not so with Jacob. He works in the smoke of the city to be sure, but he lives in the suburbs and has his own garden. His children are healthier; they go to better schools. On Sunday he packs up a picnic lunch and bundles the

45

family into the car and has a glorious day in the woods or at the beach...

"And all this is made possible by a dollar's worth of gasoline!"

What Barton did was show gasoline to be a miraculous agent for making life better for all of us. He simply "revealed the gasoline nobody knows."

The Business Nobody Knows

When big league companies such as Sears & Roebuck or Hallmark Cards sponsor television programs (an idea created by Barton), they are revealing themselves to be caring. "Brought to you by Hallmark" lets you know Hallmark is human---while also planting its name in your mind.

Bruce Barton began a book in 1928 designed to reveal business as a major force for positive change. Many people fear or flee business because they think it's corrupt. Sometimes business *is* corrupt. But Barton saw business shaping society and helping it grow. Barton's book was going to "reveal the business nobody knows." (Probably due to the Great Depression of 1929, Barton shelved the project.)

In 1957 Barton offered to help Du Pont. He said he would create new advertising that **"...would dramatize the company's research, its dependence on and interrelation with smaller** businesses, its success in managing to get along all these years without any strikes, the home life of its employees, and the tremendous contribution to the comfort and health of the American people as a result of what has gone on in the laboratories."

In short, Barton wanted to "reveal the Du Pont nobody knows."

Teach Them Why

Revealing your business means educating people about what you do.

Most businesses tell a partial story. They run a series of short ads because they believe no one will read any single long ad. But as the great copywriter Claude Hopkins declared in his famous 1923 book, *Scientific Advertising*: "People are not apt to read successive advertisements on any single line. No more than you read a news item twice, or a story....So present to the reader, when once you get him, every important claim you have."

In 1952 Barton advised the NY Stock Exchange to **"...find some way to translate their story into terms of human life and the reader's self-interest."** He also suggested that the Exchange reveal their business by pointing out they have 600 firms and 1,300 members in 73 cities; and that they are a money-saving institution.

What Barton was encouraging his clients to do was tell their whole story. He knew people would be understanding if you explained your business. Reveal the business nobody knows by telling people what you are all about. You still have to be brief, and simple, and interesting, of course. But if you tell your story, you will win more loyal customers than if you don't.

Look at it this way:

If I tell you I charge $200 an hour for my services, you might wince.

But if I explain that I require that fee because of my education, experience, and expenses; and because of the personalized rare service I deliver, and because of how much money I can help make for you, then you would feel better about my fee.

Why? Since you now have a reason why I charge what I do, you are more likely to accept the fee.

People are logical *and* emotional. You have to provide both to capture their loyalty.

The YOU Nobody Knows

Your business does more than provide a service.

Once you reveal the business nobody knows---to yourself and to your clients---you discover how business transforms life itself.

Another Barton example (from 1925):

48

"The General Electric Company and the Western Electric Company find the people in darkness and leave them in light; the American Radiator finds them cold and leaves them warm; International Harvester finds them bending over their sickles the way their grandfathers did and leaves them riding triumphantly over their fields..."

And here's Barton describing how the automobile made us lords over the earth:

"The automobile companies find a man shackled to his front porch and with no horizon beyond his own door yard and they broaden his horizon and make him in travel the equal of a King."

"I have been out of a job three times in my life. Each time I made a survey of my surroundings and discovered that there was work to be done, though not the same kind of work I had been doing."

-- Bruce Barton, 1941

"**Bruce Barton**:...Here is a man who knew Lincoln, who shook his hand, and heard his voice, and watched him laugh at one of his own funny stories. Did you feel, as you talked to him, 'I am in the presence of a personality so extraordinary that it will fascinate men for centuries...?'

"**Russell Conwell**: Not at all. He seemed a very simple man, I might almost say ordinary, throwing his long leg over the arm of his chair and using such commonplace, homey language...So it was hard to be awed in the presence of Lincoln; he seemed so approachable, so human and simple..."

-- Conversation between Bruce Barton (age 34) and Russell Conwell (age 78), author of *"Acres Of Diamonds,"* 1921

SECRET #2:

USE A GOD TO LEAD THEM

"In each generation are a few men who catch a vision so big and steadfast that in the pursuit of it they lose all thought of their own interest or advantage..."

-- Bruce Barton, 1918

Riding To Her Death

"Tonight will make history. This will be the turning point in the campaign. The General must be expertly stage managed and when he speaks, it must be with the understanding and the mercy and the faith of God."

1952. Bruce Barton was secretly guiding Dwight David Eisenhower into power. Barton was using the same strategy he used for Calvin Coolidge and later for Herbert Hoover: Barton was creating "a god to lead them."

The son of a famous minister, Barton was always drawing inspiration from religion. It's no accident that his most famous book was about Christ (and his second most famous book was about the Bible).

Barton used emotionally packed archetypes in his ads. One of his most famous ads, done quickly and almost by accident, included a sketch of Marie Antoinette "...riding to her death."

By drawing a connection to a significantly respected and emotionally charged mother-father-child figure from history, Barton was able to touch the deepest emotions of people. (And that ad pulled *eight times* better than all previous ads for the same subject: Dr. Eliot's "Five Foot Shelf" of Harvard Classics.)

The Service Guru

When Ron McCann hired me to write his book on service, Ron intuitively began to use this secret. During the process of creating *The Joy Of Service*, Ron one day announced that he was "a guru for service."

Was this his ego talking? Maybe. None of us are here without an ego. But Ron was letting people know that he was the spokesman for service. By calling himself the "service guru" he created a type of god for people to follow.

52

People love experts. Authorities are more easily listened to because we assume they know what they're talking about. It always amazes me that anyone who writes a book becomes an expert on the subject of that book---even if the book is crammed with erroneous information.

Become an authorized expert in your field and you become a type of "god." Like McCann, you establish yourself as THE person to talk to, listen to, and hire. Ron McCann's business sky-rocketed once his book came out. He became the "service guru" and everyone wanted a part of him.

Ron now travels back and forth to Mexico giving talks on service. And the book was translated into Spanish in 1991.

Become The Expert

Companies are always using celebrities in their ads because celebrities are types of gods to us. We know them, love them, respect them. If you think your favorite film star uses something, you are more inclined to buy the product. You'll follow your "god" right into the store.

It's more powerful to do what Ron McCann did. Set YOURSELF up as the expert in your field. Writing a book (or hiring someone to do it) will work. It positions you as an expert:

* Tom Peters became the expert on
  excellence when his book came out.

* Lee Iaccoca became a popular leader
  when his books became best sellers.

* Harvey MacKay's speaking career
  soared when his books hit the stands.

* And Dave Thomas, founder of *Wendy's*,
  just wrote a book on his ideas for
  achieving success.

And the businesses of every one of these people improved. (Had *you* ever heard of Harvey MacKay before he wrote a book?)

If you feel you aren't smart enough or important enough to be considered an expert on anything, consider what Bruce Barton wrote in 1920:

"Lincoln said a wonderfully wise thing one day.

'I have talked with great men,' he said, 'and I cannot see wherein they differ from others.'"

By the way, Barton's father was an expert on the life of Lincoln. He wrote several biographies of Lincoln and was considered a "god" in his field of expertise.

You probably have skills you aren't even aware

of. When I meet with clients I sit and listen to their stories. Buried within their monologue is usually a golden book idea. I point it out to them and then help them create the book. The end result is a product they can sell (the book) and a ticket to instant credibility. In addition to all that, a book is a traveling PR agent, selling you and your message even when you aren't present.

Doug Johnson's Secret

Last summer I was invited on the Doug Johnson radio show. Doug is one of the most popular media people in all of Texas. His talk show is a major hit here in Houston. It was exciting to be asked on his show. And though the show was fun, what Doug and I talked about *off* the air was even more exciting and revealing.

Doug told me he had written a novel. Since my expertise is in nonfiction, I suggested he try his hand at writing a how-to book.

"I wouldn't know what to write about," Doug said.

Now here's a talk show host with decades of experience under his belt in handling all types of people and yet he didn't see the diamond in his own backyard.

"Doug, you are an expert in dealing with people and getting them to open up," I said. "You've seen people scared stiff and yet you helped them relax. You've seen people who talked too much and yet you managed to slow them down. And you do it all with such gentleness and charm!"

"So?"

"So write a book on how to have conversations with people. Or write a book on how to talk in any situation. Or write a book on how to make people relax and open up under any circumstances. People don't know what you know, Doug!"

Then this wonderful man started to tell me some stories about people he had seen over the years.

"One woman was a sex therapist who wanted to know if she could say anything on the air," Doug recalled. "Just as we went live she asked, 'Is it okay to say *!@X%$!!?*' My face turned beet red!"

I laughed and said, "Doug, those are the stories people would love to read about. You could use them to illustrate your points."

Doug Johnson's eyes lit up.

He heard me. He was a famous talk show host, a celebrity in Texas, yet it had never occurred to him that he knew anything!

His expertise was a secret he kept from himself.

How To Create A Miracle

When Ron McCann's book was off the press and he and I were sitting in his office, resting after the long effort to create it, I said, "Ron, do you realize we've created a miracle?"

He didn't know what I meant.

"This book is going to go out into the world and be read by people you don't know, and touch people you'll never meet, and start conversations that you'll never hear," I explained. "Our book is like another life form. It will move and change lives all by itself. People will talk about it, and talk about you, and you may never know it. That's a miracle."

Bruce Barton wrote several books (all but one now out of print). They established him as an authority. At one point the offices of BBDO in New York were packed with people wanting the legendary Bruce Barton to do their ads.

Why? Because Barton was seen as a type of god. And everyone wanted a part of him. He was seen as success. And everyone wanted to see if some would rub off on them.

It's clear to me that BBDO became a famous advertising agency largely due to the fame of Bruce Barton himself. Frank Rowsome, Jr., in his delightful book, *They Laughed When I Sat Down*, said Barton was BBDO's "resident deity."

57

Barton was a best selling author, a community leader, a philanthropist, a politician, a respected authority in business. He was, in effect, a type of "god" people wanted to follow.

And Barton still lives---within the miracles of his books.

Back in 1920 Bruce Barton wrote this thought-provoking line:

"If you have anything really valuable to contribute to the world, it will come through the expression of your own personality---that single spark of divinity that sets you off and makes you different from every other living creature."

How can you establish yourself as a type of god?

Post & Crocker & Earhart

Three more quick examples for you to think about:

While working on the American Tobacco Company account, Barton suggested getting Emily Post (a clear goddess) to do an advertisement on the etiquette of smoking. ("Don't smoke in elevators. Don't light a cigarette until after the salad.")

This may come as a surprise to you, but "Betty Crocker" is a fictional character. Barton co-created her in order to lead customers to buying General Mills' products. Clearly Betty Crocker is a god well loved by the masses.

Finally, the American Tobacco Company got Amelia Earhart to promote *Lucky Strike* cigarettes in 1928 (even though Earhart did not smoke). While this example violates another Barton secret (sincerity), you can easily see that leaders are often perceived as "gods/goddesses" to the masses.

"Every man in a big position knows in his own heart that forces entirely outside himself have played a large part in his making."
-- Bruce Barton, 1928

"Many of us are afraid this expenditure of compassion will drain away our energy, deplete us for our own tasks. But the dynamics of compassion defy the ordinary laws of energy. We discover that, like Antaeus in the ancient myth, our strength is doubled by compassionate contact with the blessed earth of humanity...

"Compassion belongs to the other great band of noble virtues---tolerance, sympathy, understanding---all marching under the banner of love."

-- Bruce Barton, 1942

SECRET #3:

SPEAK IN PARABLES

"Money has a perverse habit of evading those who chase it too hard, and of snuggling up to folks who are partially unmindful of it."
-- Bruce Barton, 1928

Snap, Crackle, Pop

Bruce Barton was one of the few men in history able to write ads, essays, articles and full-length books---all with equal impact.

Part of his secret was due to his ability to write simple, snappy copy that was also rich in depth and meaning. He did this by creating stories that reached the common worker as well as the intellectuals. It's also a technique that Barton's two models, Jesus Christ and Abraham Lincoln, used to create unforgettable and highly persuasive "ads."

61

"(Jesus) told His listeners stories," Barton wrote in a private memo in 1951. **"The story, 'A certain man went down from Jerusalem to Jericho and fell among thieves.' Every one of his listeners knew some man who had fallen among thieves on that dangerous Jerusalem turnpike. They listened to the story and remembered it. If He had said, 'I want to talk to you about why you should be a good neighbor,' nobody would have listened."**

Hypnotic Stories

Stories move people. As author Jean Houston once told me, "We are storied people." We group the experiences of our lives into stories. We gossip in story format. We don't see life as a river, we see it as a story with a definite beginning, middle and end. Stories make life easier to understand.

Practitioners of NLP (neural-linguistic programming) have discovered stories are a powerful way to persuade people. Milton Erickson, the legendary hypnotist, was known for his therapeutic stories. Stories are a way for a message to be delivered indirectly.

With a story your sales message "seeps in" under the reader's awareness. If you tell someone to do something in a direct, forceful manner, they'll probably resist. But if you give the same order as a suggestion within the frame of a story, they'll probably do exactly what you want.

Let me explain:

How To Sell Bad Products

John Caples was a brilliant copywriter who worked with Bruce Barton. Maxwell Sackheim was another famous copywriter who probably knew Barton. Both of these legends had experiences that illustrate the power of "story selling."

Both of these advertising giants were assigned the task of writing ad copy for books that were actually bad. How do you sell a product that isn't any good? How would *you* do it?

Both Caples and Sackheim, working independently of each other, wrote letters that are still talked about today---*decades* after they were written. Their letters were so mesmerizing that they STILL cause those bad books to sell.

How did they do it?

They wrote their ads as stories. They talked about how they were changed by reading the book they wanted to sell. Without going into any ethical questions here, pause and consider how powerful their stories must have been.

If I told you "These shoes will make your feet feel

better" you'd shrug your shoulders and move on.

But if I told you a story about how my feet once ached so bad I cried in bed at night, and how I one day discovered a pair of magic shoes that made my feet feel like they were on air pads, you'd perk up and listen.

Why? Because I told you a story.

Story Selling

A parable is a story. Barton wrote stories laced with subtle meaning. Caples and Sackheim wrote stories that made their sales letters irresistible. Every great speaker (and Barton was an electrifying speaker) knows a good story can deliver their point better than anything else imaginable.

What are the success stories in your business?

Who bought your product or service and was transformed? Who have you worked for and made a difference? Those are your parables, the stories that sell people on what you offer.

When I was selling a software product, a customer called and said, "Joe, I was skeptical when I saw your letter about the program. But I took a chance. Boy was I surprised! I turned on my computer, the program began to talk to me, and when I was all done I had written a letter that brought me over one thousand dollars! I have the check in my hands right now."

That's a persuasive story. It's a story that also sells other people on buying the program.

When I tell people that I write books, they nod politely while thinking of what they need at the store. But when I tell a story about helping a young speaker create a book and now the speaker is traveling world-wide and getting rich, people listen.

He Died A Millionaire

When I was working up an ad to sell this book, I decided to use a "story selling" technique.

I could have written some clever ad that said this book would make you rich..and famous...and help you make money while you sleep.

I *could* have done that. But I didn't.

I decided to tell you a story....about a man who was once so famous his name was a household word..about a man who wrote a best selling book that inspired a nation to deliver service...about a man who helped create one of the largest advertising firms in the world...about a man who ate with Presidents and Kings and served in Congress...about a man who lost a wife, a daughter, a son...and died an unknown millionaire in 1967.

In short, I decided to sell you with the power of a story.

And since you are now reading this book, apparently the story selling approach worked.

A Barton Story Sells Me

One of Bruce Barton's books was the 1926 volume *What Can A Man Believe?* In it Barton tells a story that sold me on an idea---nearly *seventy years* after Barton told the story!

"Some years ago a crumpled and dejected citizen came to my office," Barton begins. The man was a sales manager with a reputation for writing sales letters. But suddenly this man was out of work and depressed. Even suicidal. Barton led the man to a window.

"Look out there at those buildings," Barton said. **"All filled with offices. Business offices. Offices of people who have goods to sell and most of whom don't know how to sell them."**

Then Barton challenged the man (another Barton tactic).

"You say you can write sales letters. This is your great chance to prove it. Write those people a letter that will sell them the idea that they need you to help them sell their goods."

The man accepted the challenge. Six months later his earnings were more than $25,000 a year---circa 1923!

That's a powerful story. When I read it, something awakened in me. I realized I could do what Barton advised that man to do. Somehow Barton's message --and his challenge--reached across seven decades and out of the pages of an old book to touch me today.

And months later, when a young copywriter came to me complaining that he couldn't get work, I led him to an open window, pointed at all the buildings outside, and told him the story I just told you.

It's the power of a parable. And it works.

A Miracle Letter

This Barton strategy helped me create one of the most celebrated letters of my career.

In 1991 I met a man who deeply influenced my life. Douglas Norment is a Houston therapist with a spiritual philosophy I respect. After only two sessions with him I sat down and wrote a sales letter for him. It's on the next page. Note how this letter is sincere (another Barton secret) and how it tells a compelling story:

****

Dear Friend,

Douglas Norment has blown my head off twice now. He's a Zen Master, Psychic Bear and Psychological Samurai--all wrapped up into a wonderfully warm and gentle fellow. Sound too hard to believe? Then get a load of this:

I've hung out with gurus, done more workshops than I care to remember, read books, written books, walked on hot coals, asked "Who Am I?" for hours on end, listened to tapes, led meditation groups, encounter groups, self-help groups, and more. I've been "on the path" for over ten years now. But nothing---**NOTHING!**---has had the sweeping and dramatic effect on my life as my sessions with Douglas.

My first experience with Douglas' "BodyMemory" work was electrifying. Under this man's wise guidance I relived past experiences and healed old hurts. Some of those "old hurts" were buried and damn uncomfortable to recall. But I let them come and I let them go. And somehow, by letting them go, there was a ripple effect that *changed everything* in my life.

Within a few days my prosperity increased. Did I say increased? My income actually and unexpectedly **DOUBLED.** Though it happened like magic, I credit Douglas' help in changing limiting beliefs to expanded ones for the miracle.

And speaking of miracles, I also transformed my relationship with my father. On Douglas' table I "breathed through" some old scenarios with my dad. Off Douglas' table I felt better about Pop. I actually missed him. Though my father is a thousand miles away, an out of state client of mine suddenly hired me for a consultation---in his state, which "just happened" to be an hour's drive from my father's house. This client also agreed to drive me to my father's home so I could drop in for a surprise visit!

Douglas' work doesn't make logical sense, however. That's why the man consistently blows my mind to smithereens and I end up, after each session, walking around "with no head." I'm sure there is a logic to Douglas' work, but it's based on *divine* wisdom, not Joe's wisdom. Don't ask me to explain it.

I encourage you to call Douglas. Tell him I sent you. Sample his medicine. And get ready for some amazing and truly wonderful changes. He's at (713) 748-7777.

Sincerely,

Joe Vitale

****

Marshall Field

During the roaring twenties Barton had numerous famous accounts. One of them was Marshall Field & Company. Most of the advertising Barton created for this popular store was based on the parable technique. For example:

"Once upon a time an obscure actor who was playing in Chicago came to Marshall Field & Company to have a pair of shoes repaired...Years later, at the height of his fame, he talked to our girls on the tenth floor..."

Another example:

"There is a man in this store who clearly remembers selling apparel to Mrs. Abraham Lincoln in 1874..."

Do you *feel* how those examples begin like stories?

Stories give color and life to your message. They involve people, entertain them, and stick with them.

What are *your* parables?

Napoleon Inspires Barton

On the last leg of my quest to learn everything I could about Bruce Barton, I flew up to Madison, Wisconsin, home of over 150 boxes stuffed with letters, articles and manuscripts by and about Barton.

70

What I noticed about Barton's writings was this: Nearly every one of his 2,000 articles and essays were in a story format. Open any article, look at the first line, and suddenly you're drawn into a story.

Barton knew stories were the best teachers---and sales people. Stories hold attention, enrich our lives, and---if they're well done---inspire and motivate us.

In one 1919 article Barton talked about Napoleon. The whole message of the piece was "Feel confident and go get a job!" But Barton *never* said that! Instead, he told a story about how his reading of Napoleon's life (a favorite Barton hero and pastime) gave him the courage and confidence to go out and *demand* a new job.

Barton absorbed the spirit of the great emperor and then hit the streets in search of work. As good stories go, this one ended happily. Barton got the job he wanted---within a wcck.

And we readers get the message---all from his delightful story.

"By a change of thought the yeoman of England became the unconquerable army of Cromwell. By a change of thought a handful of fishermen of Palestine transformed human history."

-- Bruce Barton

71

"I hope I may never be guilty of writing anything intended to make poor people contented with their lot.

"I would rather be known as one who sought to inspire his readers with a *divine discontent*.

"To make men and women discontented with bad health, and to show them how, by hard work, they can have better health.

"To make them discontented with their intelligence, and to stimulate them to continued study.

"To urge them on to better jobs, better homes, more money in the bank.

"But it does not harm, in our striving after these worth-while things, to pause once in a while and count our blessings."

-- Bruce Barton, 1920

SECRET #4:

DARE THEM TO TRAVEL THE UPWARD PATH

"People are what they are; and when you have made up your mind to that you are a long way on the road to serenity."   -- Bruce Barton, 1925

The Zest Of The Battle

Barton was almost always positive and uplifting in his ads (when he wasn't, the ads often failed) and in his books.

But he knew the value of a challenge.

Barton once suggested that there were two roads in life: one upwards, one stuck in monotony. Another of his famous ads (which ran over *seven years*) began,

73

"A WONDERFUL TWO YEARS' TRIP

AT FULL PAY---

BUT ONLY MEN WITH IMAGINATION CAN

TAKE IT."

Barton believed the great game of life was to challenge yourself to become the best you could possibly be, whether in business or at home.

He wrote, **"Whatever obstacles, whatever disappointments may come, are merely added chances against him, contributing to the zest of the contest."**

Barton knew people wanted to improve their life, but that people often didn't act in their own best interests unless prodded. His nudge was a subtle, psychological one.

A 1926 ad for washing machines pointed out that without a machine, your spouse was working for three cents an hour. **"Human life is too precious to be sold at a price of three cents an hour,"** said the ad.

It worked. The reasoning appealed to the desire of people to leave their hardships and troubles behind, and begin to move towards an easier, better lifestyle.

Another ad began,

"This book may not be intended for you—

but thousands found in it what

they were seeking."

And a proposed Campbell soup ad campaign was to begin with the headline, **"Why do you keep on bending over a hot stove to make your own soup?"**

Barton challenged the reader without insulting him. There is a fine line here.

If I write an ad that says, "You'd be a fool to pass up my services!" you would probably pass up my services.

But if I write something that begins, "Only the most dedicated achiever will use my services," then you'd probably check out what I had to say. The latter tease would challenge you by subtly asking: "Are you a dedicated achiever?"

Another Barton ad began,

"Men who 'know it all' are not invited

to read this page!"

I'd read that page. Wouldn't you? Why? Because

75

neither of us are "know it alls," right?

Again, you're being challenged.

And let's not forget the Marines. They're still looking "for a few good men." It's a challenge that still holds power (and that's why the Marines still use the ad).

Only You Should Read This

A friend recently called. She is opening a new business, an antique store, and wanted to know how to use this Barton strategy to get people to attend her grand opening.

"What can I say on my invitation to challenge them to come here?" she asked me.

We kicked around ideas for a moment. Then I offered:

"How about a headline that says, 'Are you one of the few people who can appreciate the value of rare collections?'"

That hit home for her. It clearly challenged people but didn't insult them. We all want to be part of an exclusive group. It appeals to the ego. You just have to be careful not to slap ˙anyone's face with your challenge.

When Barton was brainstorming ideas for the American Tobacco account, he offered this subtle challenge for a radio commercial:

"We believe that the people who like the finest things---fine books, fine music, fine food--are the people who should like fine tobacco. And if you are one of these people, and if you enjoy this program, and if you have not tried Luckies lately, please buy yourself two packs and smoke them. Really fine tobacco does make a difference in the taste."

And in 1953 Barton advised Schaefer beer to involve its audience. Instead of yelling the company's name, Barton suggested Schaefer become more exciting by tying the beer to popular events, such as a baseball game. Barton offered these radio ads:

"What are the chances that Joe Black will pitch a no-run game this afternoon?" and "Come over and see whether you think Jackie Robinson is playing third base as well as he played second."

Do you see how those teasers challenged listeners?

How can you challenge (but not insult) your potential clients and customers?

"Sometimes when I consider what tremendous consequences come from little things...I am tempted to think...there are no little things."

-- Bruce Barton

"Be genuine....Do not venture into the sunlight unless you are willing first to put your house in order. Emerson said, 'What you are thunders so loud I can't hear what you say.' No dyspeptic can write convincingly of the joys of mince meat. No woman-hater can write convincingly of love...

"Unless you have a real respect for people, a real affection for people, a real belief that you are equipped to serve them, and that by your growth and prosperity they will likewise grow and prosper, unless you have this deepdown conviction, gentlemen, do not attempt advertising. For somehow it will return to plague you."

-- Bruce Barton, 1925

SECRET #5:

THE ONE ELEMENT MISSING

"I believe the public has a sixth sense of detecting insincerity, and we run a tremendous risk if we try to make other people believe in something we don't believe in. Somehow our sin will find us out."
     -- Bruce Barton, 1925

Do You Support It?

Barton's writings had an element lacking in most of the other ads of the 1920's - 1940's: sincerity.

Barton's ads came across with a human, inspiring and friendly feel that people trusted. The secret was in Barton's own belief in what he was selling. If he did not support a product or service, he would not write about it. But when he did support it, his honesty came through.

79

This is an important point with me. Too many people in advertising believe you don't have to care about your product to sell it. They cite stories about John Caples and Maxwell Sackheim writing powerful letters for books they either hadn't read or considered pretty bad.

I disagree.

Who knows how powerful a letter Caples and Sackheim *could* have written had they sincerely loved (or even read) the books they were writing about? It's been my experience that when I support a cause, I can write about it much more powerfully and persuasively. If I don't support it, it shows. Customers aren't stupid.

Besides that, why would you want to sell a product you didn't use or support yourself?

The Acknowledged Master

The late John Caples was a master at writing ads. All of his books are classics (and well worth reading). Who did Caples think was better than himself? Bruce Barton!

Caples said, "Barton had the three things every writer has to have: (1) Sincerity, (2) Sincerity, (3) Sincerity."

Now the odd thing is that disciples of Caples don't agree sincerity is necessary. This attitude reeks of peddlers selling magic elixirs. Without sincerity, you're lying to your customers. It's wrong.

One famous copywriter read an early version of this book and said he didn't think sincerity was important, either. He said, "A professional writer should be like a hired assassin. No emotions. Take the product and sell it."

I nearly choked to think this leading authority felt this way about the advertising profession. His attitude reflects what I don't like in business: insincere people out for the buck.

In a sense, however, this copywriter is right. You should be skilled enough to sell anyone a product or service with the power of your words.

But again my point is this: Why would you want to sell a product or service you didn't sincerely endorse?

True Service Or Greed?

Helen Woodward was a cynical but observant business woman. She was clearly ahead of her time.

Back in 1926 she wrote in *Through Many Windows*, her autobiography, "In the old days, no one ever wrapped money-making eagerness in sweet words like *service*. Business men were frankly after money. They are still after money, but they know now that it is good policy to deliver something good to keep the customer. So they make better goods at better prices---because they have to. And they call that *service*."

Recently a new client came to me. She wanted to write a book on service. When I asked why, she said she had heard it was "in." She had little experience in delivering service and wasn't sure what service really meant, but she was convinced that writing a book on the subject would advance her career. She was right. It would advance her career. But not far. And not for long.

Without sincerity, you're selling air. Sooner or later someone (a Helen Woodward of our generation) will blow the whistle on you. You'll be exposed as a fraud. You'll lose credibility.

What Woodward saw in her generation was a bunch of businessmen who had heard that service would help them. They weren't sincerely interested in delivering service. They were sincerely interested in making money. (There's nothing wrong with making money; but it should come as a result of your service.)

Roy Durstine (the D in BBDO), in his 1921 book *Making Advertisements And Making Them Pay*, wrote, "Without sincerity an advertisement is no more contagious than a sprained ankle."

And Robert Bedner, in his 1949 senior thesis biography of Barton, wrote, "Contrary to the general belief about advertising men, Barton did regard sincerity and truth as the first essential of successful advertising."

Honesty Sells

Barton was sincere. Even Julian Lewis Watkins, while selecting several Barton ads for his book *The 100 Greatest Advertisements*, said Bruce Barton's ads were notable for their sincerity.

Though Barton often had trouble balancing his work life with his spirituality (hence his two most famous books trying to balance the two), he was earnest. And his honesty showed. It is this characteristic that attracted many people (including me) to his works.

Many studies have shown that the number one element lacking that keeps people from buying anything is trust. They've been burned too often before, by other advertisers, to trust you now.

You know this is a fact. When you read an ad, you always wonder "Is this true? Are the claims valid?" This is another reason why people read news stories **5 to 9 times more** than they reads ads. They simply don't trust advertising!

Do you believe in what you are doing or selling? If you don't, you better get into something where your heart and soul can live happily. After all, YOU are the best sales person for your business! If you aren't convinced, how are you going to excite anyone else?

Bob Bly, author of 18 business books, says in his *The Copywriter's Handbook*, "When you believe in your product, it's easy to write copy that is sincere, informative, and helpful. And when you are sincere, it comes across to the reader and they believe what you've written."

Jay Abraham, a marketing genius who charges over $3,000 an hour for his services, said: "You have to believe in your product. A product has to have a value in your heart and mind before you can passionately translate your enthusiasm to somebody else."

Bruce Barton's genuine feelings for the items or causes he represented helped him create marketing campaigns that broke all earlier records. For example:

* Barton wrote a charity solicitation letter in 1925 that brought in an overwhelming (and previously unheard of) return of well over 100%! His heartfelt letter for Berea College, sent to only 24 people, pulled in over $30,000 in contributions.

* Barton wrote a series of fund raising letters for Deerfield Academy that were so moving they were collected and sold as examples of sincere writing.

* Barton and Alex Osborn organized the United War Workers Campaign of 1918. Their goal was $175 million. Though the campaign went into effect *after* the war (World War I) ended, the sincerity of the program managed to raise over $204,000,000---the largest amount ever collected in a freewill offering in

the history of the world!

You Can Fool Them Once (Maybe)

You can't use these secrets to manipulate people into buying from you. This principle of sincerity means people will buy---or not---depending on how sincere you come across.

Clyde Bedell, in his 1940 book *How To Write Advertising That Sells*, wrote, "The best way to be sincere is---to be sincere. An attempt to write sincerity into your copy without honestly wanting to be sincere won't work."

When I wrote a sales letter to sell "Thoughtline," an artificial intelligence software program, I was totally in support of it. And my letter showed it. I got an incredible response---over 5%---in a recession. (The average sales letter gets zero to 0.02% response.)

But when I wrote a letter on another service, one which I had reservations about, my lack of support was seen by all. It was "between the lines" but still obvious.

That letter was a dud.

You can only sell what you sincerely believe in. You may be able to fool people once, but you'll lose a repeat customer. Since most of your business will come from your satisfied customers (who keep coming back for more), you can't afford to be insincere or manipulative.

Bruce David, author of *Mercenary Marketing*, says if you don't offer a product or service of true value, you won't stay in business. David openly admits, "(Advertising) may persuade people to try your products or services (as it should) once; but if you don't offer value and quality, you won't convert these people into repeat customers."

They Told Him No

Final thought on this subject: When Bruce Barton wrote his most famous book, *The Man Nobody Knows*, he had no evidence that the book would ever sell.

His friends tried to stop him. They said he wasn't an expert. They said there were already far too many books on the subject. They said it would ruin his reputation.

Barton wrote the book because of his sincere desire to share his thoughts. Robert Bedner said, "There is no doubt that the book was written out of sincere conviction."

The result was a 1925 (and 1926) best seller that is still in print today----over sixty-five years after it was written.

The magic of sincerity.

Do *you* support what you sell or do?

"The advertisements which persuade people to act are written by men who have an abiding respect for the intelligence of their readers, and a deep sincerity regarding the merits of the goods they have to sell."
-- Bruce Barton

Here is Bruce Barton's famous 1925 solicitation letter for Berea College. He sent it to 24 people. The result was a 100% return of about $30,000. It's considered one of the most effective letters ever written. See if you can detect how Barton used every one of the strategies in this book when he composed this incredible letter.

* *

Dear Mr. Blank,

For the past three or four years things have been going pretty well at our house. We pay our bills, afford such luxuries as having the children's tonsils out, and still have something in the bank at the end of the year. So far as business is concerned, therefore, I have felt fairly well content.

But there is another side to a man which every now and then gets restless. It says: "What good are you anyway? What influences have you set up, aside from your business, that would go on working if you were to shuffle off tomorrow?"

Of course, we chip in to the Church and the Salvation Army, and dribble out a little money right along in response to all sorts of appeals.

88

But there isn't much satisfaction in it. For one thing, it's too diffused and, for another, I'm never very sure in my own mind that the thing I'm giving to is worth a hurrah and I don't have time to find out.

A couple of years ago I said: *"I'd like to discover the one place in the United States where a dollar does more net good than anywhere else."* It was a rather thrilling idea, and I went at it in the same spirit in which our advertising agency conducts a market investigation for a manufacturer. Without bothering you with a long story, I believe I *have found the place.*

This letter is being mailed to 23 men besides yourself, twenty-five of us altogether. I honestly believe that it offers an opportunity to get a maximum amount of satisfaction for a minimum sum.

Let me give you the background.

Among the first comers to this country were some pure blooded English folks who settled in Virginia but, being more hardy and venturesome than the average, pushed on west and settled in the mountains of Kentucky, Tennessee, North and South Carolina. They were stalwart lads and lassies. They fought the first battle against the British and shed the first blood. In the Revolution they won the battle of King's

Mountain. Later, under Andy Jackson, they fought and won the only land victory that we managed to pull off in the War of 1812. Although they lived in southern states they refused to secede in 1860. They broke off from Virginia and formed the state of West Virginia; they kept Kentucky in the Union; and they sent a million men into the northern armies. It is not too much to say that they were the deciding factor in winning the struggle to keep these United States united.

They have had a rotten deal from Fate. There are no roads into the mountains, no trains, no ways of making money. So our prosperity has circled all around them and left them pretty much untouched. They are great folks. The girls are as good looking as any in the world. Take one of them out of her two-roomed log cabin home, give her a stylish dress and a permanent wave, and she'd be a hit on Fifth Avenue. Take one of the boys, who maybe never saw a railroad train until he was 21: give him a few years of education and he goes back into the mountains as a teacher or doctor or lawyer or carpenter, and changes the life of a town or county.

This gives you an idea of the raw material. Clean, sound timber---no knots, no worm holes; a great contrast to the imported stuff with which our social settlements have to work in New York and other cities.

Now, away back in the Civil War days, a little college was started in the Kentucky mountains. It started with faith, hope, and sacrifice, and those three virtues are the only endowment it has ever had. Yet today it has accumulated, by little gifts picked up by passing the hat, a plant that takes care of 3000 students a year. It's the most wonderful manufacturing proposition you ever heard of. They raise their own food, can it in their own cannery; milk their own cows; make brooms and weave rugs that are sold all over the country; do their own carpentry, painting, printing, horeshoeing, and everything, teaching every boy and girl a trade while he and she is studying. And so efficiently is the job done that---

a room rents for 60 cents a week (including heat and light)

meals are 11 cents apiece (yet all the students gain weight on the fare; every student gets a quart of milk a day)

the whole cost to a boy or girl for a year's study---room, board, books, etc.---is $146. More than half of this the student earns by work; many students earn all.

One boy walked in a hundred miles, leading a cow. He stabled the cow in the village, milked her night and morning, peddled the milk, and put himself through college. He is now a major in the United States Army. His brother, who owned half the cow, is a missionary in Africa. Seventy-five per cent of the graduates go back to the mountains, and their touch is on the mountain counties of five states: better homes, better food, better child health, better churches, better schools; no more feuds; lower death rates.

Now we come to the hook. It costs this college, which is named Berea, $100 a year per student to carry on. She could, of course, turn away 1500 students each year and break even on the other 1500. Or she could charge $100 tuition. But then she would be just one more college for the well-to-do. Either plan would be a moral crime. The boys and girls in those one-room and two-room cabins deserve a chance. They are of the same stuff as Lincoln and Daniel Boone and Henry Clay; they are the very best raw material that can be found in the United States.

I have agreed to take ten boys and pay the deficit on their education each year, $1,000. I have agreed to do this if I can get twenty-four other men who will each take ten. The president, Dr. William J. Hutchins (Yale 1892), who ought to be giving every minute of his time to running the college, is out passing the hat and riding the rails from town to town. He can manage to get $50,000 or $70,000 a year. I want to lift part of his load by turning in $25,000.

This is my proposition to you. Let me pick out ten boys, who are as pure blooded Americans as your own sons, and just as deserving of a chance. Let me send you their names and tell you in confidence, for we don't want to hurt their pride, where they come from and what they hope to do with their lives. Let me report to you on their progress three times a year. You write me, using the enclosed envelope, that, if and when I get my other twenty-three men, you will send President Hutchins your check for $1,000. If you will do this I'll promise you the best time you have ever bought for a thousand dollars.

Most of the activities to which we give in our lives stop when we stop. But our families go on; and young life goes on and matures and gives birth to other lives. For a thousand dollars a year you can put ten boys or girls back into the mountains who will be a leavening influence in ten towns or counties, and their children will bear the imprint of your influence. Honestly, can you think of any other investment that would keep your life working in the world so long a time after you are gone?

This is a long letter, and I could be writing a piece for the magazines and collecting for it in the time it has taken me to turn it out. So, remember that this is different from any other appeal that ever came to you. Most appeals are made by people who profit from a favorable response, but this appeal is hurting me a lot more that it can possibly hurt you.

What will you have, ten boys or ten girls?

Cordially yours,

Bruce Barton

* *

"Faith in business, faith in the country, faith in one's self, faith in other people---this is the power that moves the world. And why is it unreasonable to believe that this power, which is so much stronger than any other, is merely a fragment of the Great Power which operates the universe."

-- Bruce Barton, *What Can A Man Believe?*, 1927

"...I do believe that the one great thing we have got to find a way to do is to make it possible, in our industrial life, for the man who stands at the bench somehow to feel in what he does the same sort of satisfaction and pride which now animates and thrills the man who sits at a desk, and to make the man who stands up to his waist in a ditch, or who swings the ax beside a tree, feel that somehow there is that in the thing he does that reaches down and takes hold on things eternal, and that every swing of the pick and every stroke of the ax is not merely so much servitude, but that, in so far as that is done in a spirit of real pride and satisfaction and service, he makes himself co-worker of Almighty God in the great task of feeding and clothing and housing the world."

-- Bruce Barton, 1921 speech

"There is a wise old saying to this effect: 'A great deal of good can be done in the world, if one is not too careful who gets the credit.'

"If your object in life is to get credit, you'll probably get it, if you work hard enough.

"But don't be too much surprised and disappointed when some chap who just went ahead and did the thing, without thinking of the credit, winds up with more medals on his chest than you, with all your striving, have collected on yours."

-- Bruce Barton, *It's A Good Old World*, 1920

SECRET #6:

GIVE YOURSELF AWAY

"If a man practices doing things for other people until it becomes so much a habit that he is unconscious of it, all the good forces of the universe line up behind him and whatever he undertakes to do."

-- Bruce Barton, 1927

Money Is A By-Product

Bruce Barton was a great philanthropist.

He donated time, energy and money to a wide variety of causes. Some of his best writings were fund raising letters for colleges and organizations he sincerely believed in.

He also believed in giving something of value away in ads. Most ads contained coupons for a free book. Whatever the item, something has to be given away to start the process of receiving. Giving

97

something away gives credibility. But this strategy also makes the potential customer feel obligated to give something back.

When Barton died in 1967, his estate was worth 2.8 million dollars. But Barton did not spend his life in the pursuit of money. He was quoted as saying that he did what he loved, and the money was a by-product of good work.

That right there may be the greatest secret to prosperity.

Barton wrote, **"Get money---but stop once in a while to figure what it is costing you to get it. No man gets it without giving something in return. The wise man gives his labor and ability. The fool gives his life."**

"Selah"

Barton, a non-Jew, also supported a 1938 organization called "Selah" which was designed to establish a Jewish state in Lower California. Though the Mexican government killed that idea, Barton's support of this organization, and many other ones, showed he believed in the power of giving.

A happy by-product of this giving was the fact that it led to business offers, more publicity, national media exposure, and helped him move into politics.

Again, Barton didn't give in order to get. His

giving of time, energy and money was sincere. But that very giving led to a lot of getting.

Women & Revolution

Barton supported women's rights long before it was fashionable to do so.

In a 1927 article for *Success* magazine Barton wrote, **"(Men) have an annoying old idea that strikes me as revolting enough to make any normal woman want to commit murder---i.e., the idea that woman is merely the bearer of children, the leader of the home, the dear sweet good little thing, and after you've said that, that's that!**

"Women have a very definite place in the world---the outside world that man has so carefully reserved for himself. I see this great wide sweep of Revolution as the most refreshing thing in the century."

Barton's feelings were sincere---even when his feelings were revolutionary.

He wasn't afraid to give his thoughts away in support of something he believed in.

"No Credit Please"

Barton also wasn't afraid to not take credit for work. It was more important to have the work done, than to see that he get the glory for doing it. For example:

Barton was a ghost writer for leading businessmen (he wrote at least one speech for President Eisenhower); he wrote many pieces under assumed names (Michael Randall, David Todd, Thomas Ryan, etc.); he let a friend write a play based on an original idea and then shared authorship; he allowed his loyal secretary (of forty years) to edit and rewrite his work; he let his father (a minister) help him think through his religious books; and he let his wife do his shopping (except for books, which he chose himself).

Barton was willing to give away his control. He was willing to delegate. As he once explained in an article, **"You can get a lot done if you're not concerned about who gets the credit for it."**

Another Level Of Giving

"Giving Yourself Away" also means to be vulnerable and honest. Show who you really are---at least reveal enough of your humanness to gain credibility.

Too many business people bark about how wonderful they are. Too many advertisers claim their "amazing" product or service is THE BEST. Their theory is that you have to sell people, and blowing your own horn is the trick.

Barton knew you could gain the public's trust by letting them know you were human---which means you *may not* be the best, the brightest, or the most amazing.

When I wrote the sales letter to offer this book to my clients and customers, I of course talked about Barton, his ideas, and how the secrets have helped legends of history. But I also included a line that said this book isn't a "get-rich overnight" book. That one statement made everything else in my letter believable.

When I wrote a sales letter for a software company in California, I told all about the wonders of the program. But I was certain to include a line that gave away my honesty.

I said, "The program doesn't do your thinking for you, but it does help you think better by joining forces with your own mind."

That one apparently "weak point" made every other point in my letter believable.

The Front Porch

Bruce Barton used this secret (and two others) when he wrote a "front porch" interview with Calvin Coolidge, President of the U.S. in the roaring '20's.

The common belief at the time was that people were interested in the politics of politicians. Sounds logical, right? But Barton had a hunch that people were more interested in people; the human qualities of politicians, and especially of the President.

Barton interviewed Coolidge. They spoke of personal interests, family, and other non-political subjects. Barton "revealed the President nobody knows," showed Coolidge's sincerity, and "gave something away"---he gave away the President's mask of power.

The newspaper reporters of the day were jealous and angry. But the public---the voters---loved it.

Earnest Elmo Calkins, another pioneer in advertising, wrote: "The public was more deeply moved to learn how the President did his shopping, or that when he was up home in the country he liked to putter around and fix the lock on the woodshed door, exactly as you or I, than to learn his views on Farm Relief or the World Court. In short, they were more interested in the President as a human being than as a politician or a statesman."

Bruce Barton's historic interview simply "gave

102

something away" to the people: humanness.

How Giving Led To Greatness

BBDO Batten, Barton, Durstine and Osborn---one of the largest ad agencies in the world (ranked sixth in 1991) began as a result of this very secret.

In 1918, after the first U.S. World War, Bruce Barton donated his talents to the United War Workers Campaign. He helped promote various charities, including the Salvation Army. (Barton coined their famous slogan, "A man may be down but he's never out.")

It was during this work that Barton met Alex Osborn and Roy Durstine (the O and D in BBDO). They became friends. Osborn persuaded Barton to form an agency with Durstine. On January 2, 1919, the agency of Barton and Durstine opened with 14 employees.

In August of the same year Osborn joined the firm. By 1925 BDO was the fifth largest ad firm in the country. In 1928 the firm merged with the George Batten Company and became BBDO---with Bruce Barton as President.

And this now legendary advertising agency, with offices all over the world and thousands of employees, began from an act of charity!

If Bruce Barton had not contributed his time and

energy to the War Workers Campaign, if he had not given himself away for a cause he sincerely believed in, the BBDO agency may never have been created.

Top This

Bruce Barton gave himself away to a staggering roster of worthy causes---and this is not a complete list!
* National Chairman, United Negro College Fund
* Publicity Committee, National Urban League
* National Chairman, American Heart
Association
* PR Committee, Salvation Army
* Fund Raising, Deerfield Academy
* President, Institute For the Crippled & Disabled
* Fund Raising, Berea College

What are *you* giving?

"Until a man is old enough to lose the idea that the purpose of life is self-entertainment, until he quits trying to entertain himself and begins trying to entertain other people, he is bound to be restless and unhappy. You must forget yourself in order to please yourself."
    -- Bruce Barton, *On The Up And Up*, 1929

"Say to yourself: 'Here I am, a human being just a little different from any who has ever lived before or will ever live again. I don't have 100 per cent equipment by any means. There are some notable lacks in my make-up, and no notable points of strength. But this is the hand that has been dealt me in the game, and I must play it. And I shall be judged not by what I accomplish in contrast with other men, but by what I make of myself in comparison with what I might have made....'"

-- Bruce Barton, 1921

"The greatest educational force in modern life is advertising...

"I said to this country doctor, 'There are five of you doctors in town; how much do you make?' He said, 'Two are starving and the other three are just barely getting along.' I said, 'Is there any cooperation among you?'

"He said, 'Not on your life. I hardly dare to take a vacation, because I am afraid the other doctors will steal my customers.' I said, 'If you would join together, spend a little money every week in advertising, if you would sell this community on the necessity of having an annual or semi-annual examination, if you would sell the community on the importance of having proper dental care in the schools and having regular health supervision of the children in the schools, you would all make more money and the community would be immeasurably in your debt.'"

-- Bruce Barton, in *Masters Of Advertising Copy*, 1925

SECRET #7:

SHARPEN THE KNIFE

"When we are through changing---we are through." -- Bruce Barton

Spit Polished

Everything Barton wrote was polished to perfection. He knew you had to "sharpen the knife" of persuasion by rewriting, testing, getting feedback, and being flexible.

During the 1930's, when Barton's name was a household word and businessmen were lining up at the doors of BBDO to have the famous writer "do their ads," Barton was wise enough to get help. He wrote many ads himself. Many others were done by the other "Bruce Bartons" hired to do the work. Yet the real Barton always supervised and revised every word until the ad was honed to perfection.

Why?

Because Barton knew that your best work comes after you've revised it. The great literary stylist E.B.

White said there was no great writing, only great re-writing.

Barton once wrote that most writers start writing something before they start SAYING something. Editing is your opportunity to be sure you've created an ad that is irresistible.

In 1920 Barton said Horace Greeley, the legendary newspaper man, **"...used to say that the way to write a good editorial was to write it to the best of your ability, then cut it in two in the middle and print the last half."**

Most of the great advertising giants from the roaring twenties and beyond knew it was wiser to create 25 headlines before settling on one. (Barton actually often created *over one hundred* headlines and selected one from the list.)

They often wrote several different ads before deciding which would work best. They all knew the value of this secret: honing your work until it was perfect.

Make It Tight

Barton was no exception. It's said that he was a stickler when it came to writing. He always wanted the copy tight. A running joke was that when he died his headstone would say, "The copy should be shorter."

Simplify and tighten your ads, your talks, your letters, and your meetings, until they squeak with tense power. Brevity is the key.

"Two men spoke at Gettysburg on the same afternoon during the Civil War," Barton wrote in 1920. **"One man....the leading orator of his day...made a 'great' oration....**

"The other speaker read from a slip of paper less than 300 words. His speech---Lincoln's Gettysburg Address---will live forever."

Even Lincoln knew the power of a few well chiseled words.

Smart Ads

Far too many business people admire "creative ads" rather than asking if the ads pull in business. Cuteness and cleverness do not usually work.

The 1991 ads for Isuzu automobiles are a perfect example. The ads won awards for their humor and originality. But did they sell cars? No. Isuzu was often *dead last* in terms of car sales.

Your focus should be on ads that work; on ads that get the results you want. That happens when you "sharpen the knife" of persuasion.

People usually ask themselves (unconsciously) three basic questions when they look at your ads: "Who cares? So what? What's in it for me?"

109

When I was working on a title for this book, I thought I'd call it "The Secrets Of Bruce Barton." But people would say "Who cares?" because they wouldn't recall Barton.

Then I thought I'd try "The Strategies Of A Forgotten Ad Man." But people would say "What's in it for me?"

I also thought I'd title the book "Bruce Barton: A Biography." But people would say "So what?" since they wouldn't know who Barton was.

The current title speaks to what people want. By sharpening the knife I was able to come up with a much stronger title.

Bruce Barton once told this story about sharpening the knife to make an advertisement more powerful:

"The human being from Adam's day to the present has been interested first of all and most of all in himself. My firm once took over the advertising of a life insurance company and has handled it now for many years. When we took it over every insurance man would tell you that the strongest appeal you could make in insurance would be to show the picture of an attractive young widow with a couple of pretty children at her knee and the photograph of her deceased husband in her hand...with some headline as 'Wasn't daddy wonderful to take out life insurance to protect us?'

110

"We began using that appeal but soon found that there was a much stronger appeal. We cut the widow and children out of the illustrations; instead we showed a happy-faced man of 65 sitting on a rock, with a brier pipe in his mouth and an old felt hat on his head, saying: 'He doesn't have to do a lick of work, and every month gets a check for $200.'

"The self-interest appeal (the desire to enjoy life and live longer) out-pulled the wife and child appeal by about 10 to 1."

Healing Knives

Since the image of a knife may cause you to shudder, let me tell you why I'm using it.

A knife can cut. A knife can kill. But a knife can also heal. Surgeons use knives to help you live.

"Sharpen the knife" doesn't mean to get ready to maim your customers. It means get ready to SERVE your customers by sharpening your advertisements and marketing strategies so they do what you want them to do: bring in new business.

Sharpen Your Choices

This strategy is also a reminder to sharpen your decisions.

111

I play the harmonica. Though I'm not Charlie Musselwhite or Howard Levy, I'm not bad, either. I play in a band from time to time, and I practice with friends.

Sounds innocent enough, doesn't it?

But I've noticed some problems.

Trying to devote my life to being an author *and* to being a musician is nearly impossible. Both careers require time. And commitment. And neither allow for "side line" activities. If I try to do both, I do *neither* very well.

On the days I try to write after staying up the night before playing music, I'm a flop. I can't get anything done. My head is too fuzzy.

And on the evenings when I try to blow my harp after writing and seeing clients all day, I'm too tired to hit a right note.

Hobbies and relaxing past times are fine. But trying to chase *two* massive dreams isn't smart.

Bruce Barton was the first to help me realize I had to sharpen my decisions. In 1920 he wrote an essay called "Slide Lines" which ended as follows:

"J.C. Penney told me the other day about a young man who might have been one of his first partners. The young man played the trombone and was compelled to leave the store early every night because he made five dollars a week by tooting his horn in an orchestra. He is still tending store in the daytime and tooting at night.

112

Mr. Penney is the head of more than eight hundred stores.

"There are men who have made fortunes by running bootblack stands, by buying junk from automobile factories, and even by contracting with a city to collect its garbage. Almost any business seems to be a good business if a man gives it all he's got.

"But the side line is the slide line."

Act Before It's Too Late

This strategy also refers to your life.

It was the July 1, 1991 death of actor Michael Landon that drove this point home for me. His sudden passing made me aware that you have to do what you know to do NOW---today---before it's too late. Our time here is limited. Landon was one of the most robust people I've ever seen. He was strong and healthy and full of life. But that didn't make him immune to dying.

Bruce Barton's life roared during the 1920's through 1950's. He was healthy and alive. But he lost a son, a daughter, a wife. He had a stroke. And by 1967, the year of his death, illness had wiped out his memory. He died nearly helpless and, except for a few friends and relatives, almost completely alone.

If Barton had not written the books he did, when

113

he did, our world would have suffered an incalculable loss. If Michael Landon had not written and starred in the shows he did, our lives would have a mysterious hole in them.

"Sharpening The Knife" is a strategy that applies to you personally. This book may have prompted some ideas in you. Are you going to take action? Are you going to do what you know to do?

If you knew your work would touch people in the same way as the work of Bruce Barton, or Michael Landon, would you act today?

Bruce Barton wrote, **"It's only when we are stirred by a great demand, an insistent necessity, that we accomplish the sort of things that make us proud of our humanity."**

That demand has to come from you. YOU have to sharpen the knife of your own being. Runners call it exceeding "Your Personal Best." Instead of competing against anyone, you run to improve yourself, to better your last score.

Are you "sharpening the knife" that is you?

"If you are going to do anything you must expect criticism. But it's better to be a doer than a critic. The doer moves; the critic stands still, and is passed by.

"You must believe in something---in yourself, in the country, in God. You must have courage to back that belief with your money and your life, and patience to wait for fulfillment."

-- Bruce Barton, 1932

INSTANT ACCESS TO THE 7 LOST SECRETS

The First Secret: Reveal The Business Nobody Knows

What are you REALLY in the business of delivering? What universal need are you fulfilling? Look past the obvious.

The Second Secret: Use A God To Lead Them

Can you establish yourself as an expert in your field? Can you write a book about your service?

The Third Secret: Speak In Parables

What are your stories? Who has bought from you and prospered or changed? Learn to use "story selling" methods.

The Fourth Secret: Dare Them To Travel The Upward Path

How can you challenge your customers without insulting them? Think of the Marines.

The Fifth Secret: The One Element Missing

Do you sincerely believe in what you are doing and selling? If not, why not?

The Sixth Secret: Give Yourself Away

What are you giving to your clients? To the world?

The Seventh Secret: Sharpen The Knife

Are you polishing your writings, your ads, until they are perfect? Go for effectiveness rather than cleverness. Are you polishing *yourself?*

Author Joe Vitale
(Photo Courtesy Andrews Photograpy)

ABOUT JOE VITALE

Joe Vitale, President of Awareness Publications, is one of the most persuasive writers alive today.

He writes sales letters, articles, and books that persuade, compel and motivate people. He is the author of several books, including *Turbocharge Your Writing*, *Zen And The Art Of Writing*, and (as coauthor) *The Joy Of Service*.

Joe is a powerful and inspiring speaker, as well as a certified direct marketing specialist.

"Joe writes as he teaches: Clear, concise, with impact...His consultations saved me 100's of hours and months of work...He knows how to inspire you."
-- Richard B. Austin, Jr., Ph.D.

"Your writing skills have helped me and my company. Your talent is a gift." -- David Perlick, President, Super Star Rent-A-Car

"I have never seen anyone write with such impact. He has an extraordinary way of capturing people's attention through the written word." -- Donna Vilas, Coauthor, *Power Networking!*

Joe Vitale * PO Box 300792 * Houston 77230-0792

CALL (281) 999-1110

119

RESOURCES

<u>Bruce Barton</u>

The only book by Barton still in print is his classic best seller, *The Man Nobody Knows* (MacMillan, 1987). However, this recent version is heavily edited. I suggest you look in old book stores for a copy of the 1925 original (it's not hard to find).

Here is a complete list of Bruce Barton's books, many of which are nearly impossible to obtain except through interlibrary loan:

Better Days (1924)
The Book Nobody Knows (1926)
He Upset The World (1931)
It's A Good Old World (1920)
The Making Of George Groton (1918)
The Man Nobody Knows (1925)
More Power To You (1917)
On The Up And Up (1929)
The Resurrection Of A Soul (1912)
What Can A Man Believe? (1927)
The Young Man's Jesus (1914)

All of Barton's letters and articles (thousands of them) and other materials are on file at The State Historical Society in Madison, Wisconsin.

There are several excellent unpublished papers on Barton:

Bruce Barton And The Twentieth Century Menace Of Unreality by Edrene Stephens Montgomery. Ph.D. dissertation. University of Arkansas. 1984. (Contains an excellent bibliography.)

And There Arose A New King Which Knew Not Joseph: A Biography of Barton by Robert Bedner. Senior thesis. Princeton. 1947.

The Messiah Of Business: A Study Of Bruce Barton by John F. Cook. Master's thesis. University of Wisconsin. 1962.

Bruce Barton: Editor, Author, Executive by Joseph Meacham. Master's thesis. University of Wisconsin. 1964. (Probably the best and most complete biography of Barton.)

The Big Sell: Attitudes Of Advertising Writers About Their Craft In The 1920's And 1930's by S. R. Shapiro. Ph.D. dissertation, University of Wisconsin, 1969. Includes a section on Barton.

Bob Bly

Write for a complete catalog of books, special reports and tapes by this prolific advertising genius. Bob Bly, 174 Holland, New Milford, NJ 07646.

John Caples

This legendary copywriter left some priceless books. His most recent may be the best: *How To Make Your Advertising Make Money* (Prentice-Hall, 1983). His earlier book, *Making Ads Pay*, contains a couple of charming stories about Bruce Barton's ads.

Ron McCann

Ron (the "Service Guru") and I wrote an inspiring book called *The Joy Of Service*. Available from SIS Publications, 10707 Corporate Drive, Suite 101, Stafford, TX 77477.

Joe Vitale

For information on my other books and services, drop me a line. Joe Vitale, PO Box 300792, Houston, TX 77230. Phone: (281) 999-1110 or Fax (281) 999-1313.

Dottie Walters

To get a copy of Dottie's excellent book, *Speak & Grow Rich*, or to get a copy of her magazine, write: Dottie Walters, PO Box 1120, Glendora, CA 91740.

Recommended Reading:

Only Yesterday: An Informal History Of The 1920's by Frederick Lewis Allen. An entertaining and educational 1931 work. Brilliant. (Perennial Library/Harper & Row, 1964.)

Scientific Advertising and My Life In Advertising by Claude Hopkins. One of advertising's founding fathers tells his secrets in two classics from the 1920's. Worth memorizing. (NTC Business Books, 1990.)

My First Sixty-Five Years In Advertising by Maxwell Sackheim. Out of print but worth hunting down. Insightful.

John Caples: ADMAN by Gordon White. (Crain Books, 1977) Only biography of direct mail king Caples. Includes brief sections on Barton.

100 Top Copywriters And Their Favorite Ads edited by Perry Schofield. (Printers' Ink, 1954). Barton's work is of course included.

The Virgin Queene by Harford Powell, Jr. (Little Brown, 1928). Novel with the main character---"Barnham Dunn"---probably based on Bruce Barton. (The author had worked for Barton.)

The 100 Greatest Advertisements edited by Julian Watkins. (Dover, 1959). A classic. Barton's work is in here several times.

How To Use Psychology For Better Advertising by Melvin Hattwick. A 1950 gem (Prentice Hall), long out of print. If you find an extra copy, tell me!

The Mirror Makers: A History Of American Advertising And Its Creators by Stephen Fox. (Vintage, 1985). Fascinating in depth look at advertising---including Barton's contribution.

Poor Richard's Legacy by Peter Baida. (Morrow, 1990). Very readable introduction to the history of business values. Includes material on Barton.

For more information
on Joe Vitale,
contact:

www.mrfire.com

"...ideas are about the cheapest of all commodities...But the supply of men who can execute ideas and make money out of them is pitifully small."

-- Bruce Barton, 1936